Introduction

In recent years I have noted how other art forms have become so streamlined and simplified that even beginning students can complete a work of art in a relatively short time. Since time is in short supply for all of us in this fast paced modern world, I have been concerned that the art of porcelain painting must also be simplified in order to attract the younger working people of today. To that end I have been developing and teaching methods to complete a design on a porcelain piece in one painting. My previous books "Florals and Fruit" and "Ramblin thru Roses" will complement this material. The use of fingers along with brushes is another simplification that has merit.

The beginnings for this book occurred quite casually some years ago. I found myself reaching across the table and using my fingers to assist a student in correcting her work. As I experimented I discovered that a stroke of the finger would simplify a wipe out which often required numerous strokes of the brush. This simplified wipe out method has won wide acceptance by both the novice and the experienced painter.

I have found over the years that my finger has become a most useful tool complementing the brush in accomplishing certain effects in my painting. It is my hope as you study the methods I have shared, that it will encourage you to develop even more ways you can use your fingers as you practice on the plastic sheets which have been included. There are many flowers and some fruits that are enhanced by the use of the fingers in addition to the few I have described. Happy painting!

SLIP AND SLIDE BRUSH STROKE

This stroke is used to lay in a heavy application of the flower color from which the finished flower(s) will be formed. This stroke may be used for foliage areas and for many flowers that do not lend themselves to the finger wipe out method. The name of the stroke is derived from the fact that the brush never leaves the painting surface until additional color must be added to the brush.

To facilitate the heavy application of paint, you will need to mix your paints very dry with Art-aide (our all purpose open medium) to a consistency similar to pie dough. This will then enable you to use more medium when you are loading your brush and working as much paint into your brush as it will hold. The medium is the agent that allows the brush to absorb the paint and lets it flow evenly from the brush to the painting surface without pulling or skipping. Do not allow your colors to puddle by using too much medium. The paint should glisten without puddling to avoid problems during firing.

The slip and slide strokes are formed by using the left corner of your brush bent forward, increasing and decreasing pressure slightly will create a petal-like effect. Start in the center of the flower area and overlap the strokes, turn the china and leave windows until the flower area is completed (see work page and practice on the plastic overlay to duplicate the strokes shown.) On some flowers such as violets and lilacs you will need to soften and trail out some of the outer edges for a more natural appearance (see work page.)

VIOLETS

SUPPLIES USED:

All purpose Betty's ART-AIDE mixing and painting medium.
Brushes: 3/4" Shader, #1 Liner, #10/0 Liner.
Colors: Lemon Yellow, Corn, Pretty Pink, Mallard, French Mauve, Azure Blue, Old Gold
Green, Chartreuse, Black Green, Cherry Red, Pretty Violet, Black, Sapphire Blue
and Betty's Enamel.

All these violets are done on a wet background--Lemon Yellow for the sunlight color, Corn for the reflected light, Mallard and Pretty Pink for accent colors. (Example see work page.) This flower is done with a "slip and slide stroke". Condition brush with ART-AIDE. Have enough paint and medium to develop heavy application that will give texture. Side load 3/4" brush with French Mauve to create the flower area. With ART-AIDE the build up will not chip and will flatten out in firing. It is important that the outer edge or area of the "slip and slide stroke" will appear to be petals. The outer edge may need some small undeveloped flowers in the background. Use Azure Blue and trail out some small "slip and slide strokes". Do this by using only the tip left corner of your brush tilted forward and filter shadow petals. Make them lacy. For a casual approach to painting a leaf. Side load your brush with Chartreuse all the way across the brush and Black Green on 1/2 the left side and tuck the back part of the leaf up under the area where your primary violets are going to be wiped out. Lay in an inverted "V" shape, start next to and cut into the flower area using the "joined diamond strokes", (see work page) then lift up on your brush, come out and a tip will form a soft leaf (see work page). Now with the leaves in let's make stems also. Use a #1 French Liner with Old Gold Green. Lay brush down in the flower color and pull out, not in a straight line but a curve for stems--the same for a bud stem except put a hook on the end.

Now let's begin wiping out. I have shown on one of the color pages how to wipe it out. Make the two top petals; practice first in some wet paint. Use your index finger, which has the deepest imprint of your finger print, (this will be the veins and whiskers). Using the ball of your finger, lay it down lightly on the surface of the paint. Stroke it ever so lightly, as you begin the movement begin to release the pressure of your finger and glide off as you reach the throat area. Using the index finger wipe out the other top petal, begin by pulling it toward what would be the throat and curve it slightly. Turn the china piece, using your finger make a short little side petal toward the throat. If you pull it in too far and it's not too noticeable just leave it alone for the time being. Turn the china and repeat the same finger motion always pulling toward the throat and do the other side petal. To do the bottom and wider petal roll the finger a bit more to the side to allow more surface contact but with the same pressure and pull toward the throat. Using the wipe out tool, make a little diamond shape that will kind of break up that overlapping of petals and create a throat. After all the petals are formed, use a semi-soft tool, one that will let you press and release and you get a thin or thick line. Start with top petals at the throat and pull out toward the tip of the petal a thin line. Some of the violets, when they first open have a slight pleat at the top two petals, this is made with a little short stroke with the wipe out tool, making sure that the strokes never connect (see work page). Do the two main petals first, then the side petals, then the bottom petal. Fill in the diamond shape throat with a thin mixture of Betty's Enamel that has been tinted with

Lemon Yellow with a heavy stroke that will leave a crease into which Cherry Red can be applied. To paint in the buds, moisten finger with medium and in a circular motion pick up Azure Blue and Pretty Violet and lightly pull the color toward the stem making a bud. Sufficient medium should be used to avoid sticking or skipping. Remember to add the sepal. You may wish to use the plastic overlay and practice over the work page before you begin wiping out. Fire at 016 or hotter.

The violets are shown on a limoges oval box. Apply wet background following instructions above. Complete the flowers, leaves and buds. For easier handling it can be fired at this point to cone 016 or hotter.

The outer edge is done in Pretty Violet, Sapphire Blue and Black. The light area is Azure Blue. Wipe out the scroll work, fire at 016 or hotter, then go back over it with an outline of Enamel, fire at 016 or hotter.

After firing you may feel that too much color has been wiped out. To give your painting more sparkle, separate thin washes of Lemon Yellow, Mallard and Pretty Pink should be applied in the wipe out areas. Try not to muddy your colors; the washes should be clear and transparent.

B. Humphrey

8

9

THE GERANIUM

SUPPLIES USED:

    All purpose Betty's ART-AIDE mixing and painting medium.

    Brushes: 3/4" Shader, #1 Liner.

      Colors: Cream, Lemon Yellow, Corn, Mallard, Pompadour Red, Red Grape, Pretty Plum, Azure Blue, Old Gold Green, Chartreuse, Black Green, Chrome Green, Autumn Green, Cherry Red and Misty Grey.

This is a "one fire" finger wipe out using "slip and slide strokes".

Do a wash of Cream to create a tint over the entire surface. This should not be fired as you will paint wet on wet. Your brush should have enough medium on it so that it will glide easily without dragging, pulling or skipping. Use accent colors of Mallard and Pretty Plum in areas around where geraniums will be placed.

Sketch in the design. With a 3/4" shader side loaded with Cherry Red the geraniums are formed using the "slip and slide brush stroke" (refer to work page). Do a series of these strokes to complete the head of each geranium. Reload your brush every 4 or 5 brushstrokes. The outer edges should be uneven to look like small petals. Lay in background colors of Chartreuse and Black Green under the main geranium. Soften the outer edges of the Black Green with Azure Blue and a little bit of Chrome Green. Lay in sunlight colors (Lemon Yellow, Corn) from upper left to lower right. Accent colors are Azure Blue and Pretty Plum. Use Old Gold Green to paint small stems connecting flowerlets to main stem. Stems are Autumn Green with a touch of Cherry Red.

For the primary leaves side load 3/4" brush with Chartreuse, Black Green and Cherry Red. Pivot around center of leaf alternating heavy and light pressure on the brush. This gives a ruffled look. The other leaves are painted the same way, but vary the colors. The leaves that are in the background lose more of the detail.

Look at the worksheet to review the strokes. Very lightly and carefully with the index finger touch the paint and pull to the center. Gradually release pressure as you approach the center. Generally geranium petals are larger than violet petals but both are formed using the same finger stroke. All you want to do is take enough color off the end so that some of the darker color is pulled toward the throat. Remember that if you can use your index finger, it has the deeper indentations from your finger prints and will act as veins for your petals. Use a wipe out tool and outline the main flowerlets, careful so as to look delicate, wipe out diamond shape for the throat, use Lemon Yellow and a touch of Red Grape for center. Where deeper color is needed use Pompadour Red and a touch of Red Grape, this appears as shadow areas.

The shadow flowers at the top are done with Azure Blue, a little bit of Chrome Green and some of the Cherry Red added to it, possibly no centers showing. Now to fill negative areas paint in shadow branches and stems, use Misty Grey. Come back in and show the buds that never completely blossom out. Fire at 016 or hotter.

You may find it easier to practice the strokes and wipe outs on the plastic overlay over the work page before actually starting to paint.

Betty Humphrey • 2804 E. Kessler Blvd. • Indianapolis, IN 46220 U.S.A.

B. Humphrey

FOUR ONE FIRE FLOWERS DONE WITH YOUR FINGERS

It may be easier for you to control the finger wipe outs on a larger plate, hence I suggest you enlarge all these designs to fit an 8" painting surfaces.

Poppies: Again a wet background of Lemon Yellow, Corn and accent colors of Mallard and Pretty Plum, which is a lovely background color with the cherry red poppies. Sketch in poppies. Dip your index finger in medium and pick up a heavy load of Cherry Red. For a variation and/or shadows use Pompadour Red. Come back in with the finger laid a little bit sideways and using side of the ball, lay in the back side of the poppy pulling toward the center. Remembering the left and right sides of the petals are curved slightly, also overlapping your finger strokes. Try not to lose the lines from your finger prints. However, you may want to use a brush to form overlapping petals. The poppy is a very crepe papery, tissuey flower and the more your lines show from your finger prints the prettier it will be. Remember pull your finger toward the center or the throat of the flower. The center of the throat of the poppy is its most unique feature and consists of a button of 1/2 Chartreuse and 1/2 Black Green. Side load a 3/4" square shader with Pretty Violet and Black and lay in color around this button. Complete poppies using finger to paint in petals always pulling toward the throat. Use your brush to define the petals wherever necessary. Use finger nail or the handle of the wipe out tool and knock out the little seeds. For leaves side load 3/4" brush with Chartreuse and Old Gold Green, (shape the petals as you fill in foliage) start next to flower, show only a portion of the leaves. Cherry Red can be used as an accent color on the leaves. Stems are done in Old Gold Green. Use a #1 french liner with enough medium in the brush so that it will glide smoothly without skipping or pulling. Hold the liner like a pencil and paint in stems. I did the bud with my finger by picking up medium and Old Gold Green.

Don't forget to include the hairlike things on the stems and also on the buds. You might split one bud showing some flower color. Leaves are soft shadowy filter strokes, it will almost make your leaves without having to work at painting leaves. You may want to use the plastic overlay and practice over the work page before you begin wiping out. Fire 016 or hotter.

SUPPLIES USED:
All purpose Betty's ART-AIDE mixing and painting medium.
Brushes: 3/4" Shader, #1 Liner.
Colors: Lemon Yellow, Corn, Pretty Plum, Mallard, Pretty Violet, Pompadour Red, Old Gold Green, Chartreuse, Black Green, Cherry Red and Black.

DAISIES: The one fire daisies are done on a wet background of Lemon Yellow, Corn and Pretty Pink. Sketch in the center of the daisy in the oval or round shape. Paint in the centers with a side load of Corn and Sienna using a 3/4" shader. Small amounts of Cherry Red, Rich Brown can be placed around the edge of the centers. Rather than paint in individual petals lay in a solid area around the centers. For this side load your brush with Azure Blue and Pretty Pink. When you begin your wipe out, remember to lay your finger down with light pressure and pull toward the center. For long petals, start out a little bit farther and pull toward the center, if they are supposed to be short then don't go too far out. Be careful not to disturb the centers. When all the petals are wiped

out with your finger, go back with a clean square shader and refine them. You may want to wipe out a little more color than you were able to get with your finger or in some cases you may have to add a little color to them. Some petals are curled up over the center, there are some petals that are overlapping the others, some petals are flat and others have points on the ends. Let's get a variety of shapes on the daisy petals. Also you can finish shaping the flowers by putting in your leaves. Side load your brush with Old Gold Green and Autumn Green and shape the petals by using the diamond stroke between the petals. Filter in accent colors in and around your daisies. This is the opportunity to shape the petals. In darker areas use Mallard Shadow and Black Green and filter in shadow leaves. Use a #1 liner with enough medium, holding it sideways pull out some stems. You may wish to use the plastic overlay and practice over the work page before you begin wiping out. Fire at 016 or hotter.

SUPPLIES USED:
    All purpose Betty's ART-AIDE mixing and painting medium.
    Brushes: 3/4" Shader, #1 Liner.
      Colors: Lemon Yellow, Corn, Cherry Red, Rich Brown, Pretty Pink, Azure Blue, Sienna, Black Green, Old Gold Green, Autumn Green and Mallard Shadow.

YELLOW WILD ROSES: For a wet background use Lemon Yellow, Corn, Pretty Pink, Pretty Plum and a touch of Mallard. Paint in the centers using Lemon Yellow, Corn and a touch of Sienna. Casually lay this in, you don't want a hard round center, just a very soft center. Then take a wipe out tool and let's pick out that little indentation in the center. You can surround that with a little bit of Rich Brown. Paint in colors for the petals. For the yellow wild rose, side load Lemon Yellow, Corn and Sienna. Lay the dark side of your brush next to the center and begin to shape the center, lay in flower petals. Using background colors shape the outer edges of petals using the "diamond and joined diamond" strokes. In the foliage area filter brush away from the rose. As you walk it out, can you begin to see shapes of leaves? Don't disturb those, keep them and use them later. Using index finger and lay it sideways and start at the outer tip of the petal and pull toward that throat, trying not to destroy the throat. It may take two or three strokes in order to complete a petal. Try to stroke it as few times as possible. Take a clean brush; shape petals and you may want to wipe out an area that has a straight edge that can make a roll back, painting a little darker color under the wipe out. If you have a white area showing, take a thin load of Pretty Pink, place it on the outer edges of those petals and kind of give the wild rose a pinkish cast in certain parts of the petals. For a break between petals, put a petal separation of Black Green using the same brush stroke as if you were making a thorn. Let's do the guard petals which are the ones that roll upward and protect the center. Try not to make them all the same size and shape.

The stems generally are put in before the leaves so that you can lay the leaves across the stems, they are made of Old Gold Green with Cherry Red using a #1 liner. Now let's form the leaves, a good color is Old Gold Green, Autumn Green and an accent of Corn, Cherry Red or Sienna on some of the leaves. Using Cherry Red, Rich Brown and Chrome Green scatter some pollen on the petals along the edges of the centers. Fire at 016 or hotter.

It will help you to use the plastic overlay on the work page to practice before you actually start painting.

SUPPLIES USED:

All purpose Betty's ART-AIDE mixing and painting medium.
Brushes: 3/4" Shader, #1 Liner.
Colors: Lemon Yellow, Corn, Pretty Pink, Mallard, Pretty Plum, Old Gold Green, Black Green, Chrome Green, Cherry Red, Sienna and Rich Brown.

ONE FIRE IRIS: You may want to study the work page where I've shown how to do this before you actually start painting. Prepare a wet tinted background of Lemon Yellow, Corn and Pretty Pink with touches of Mallard. Use Azure Blue, Sapphire Blue and Pretty Violet for the flower color. Let's do the standards first. You may use a brush or you can put some medium on your finger and pick up Azure Blue and a little bit of the Sapphire Blue and some of the Pretty Violet and actually stroke on the iris, whichever is easiest for you. Paint the standards by pulling toward the center veins working upward to tip and down the other side to where it goes into the stem. The falls start out at the end of the petals and work into where they go into the main part of the flower. Before refining the iris paint in leaves using Chrome Green and a touch of Black Green. Start at the bottom, lay brush at an angle and pull up to the flower and continue the leaf above the petals and release the pressure on the brush as you get out to the tip, it becomes thinner and to a point. You can change the colors and size of your leaves. To vary the color of the leaves use Olive Green and Chartreuse as you feel appropriate. Come back in and put a stem for the bud using Old Gold Green and a #1 liner. With medium on your finger and some flower color form the bud by making a slight "C" starting at the base of the bud and working to the end. Put casings around portions of that bud using Cream and Chrome Green. Now we are ready to wipe out the flower itself. Use clean index finger, no medium, lay it down at the bottom part of the main petals next to the throat and work upward and overlap finger strokes toward center vein by the movement of your finger. Barely lay your finger on the surface of the paint stroking it toward the center vein. You will do the other side the same way and you'll see a natural vein begin to form, This may act as a very soft vein. There are quite a few streaks of color coming out of that main vein. You may want to add some color to those veins, or you may want to use a clean brush and lift some out if it is too dark, also refine the outer edges of the petals. Turn the china to be more comfortable in doing the falls which are done with a similar stroke as the standards. Wipe out areas for the beards. Use a thin mixture of Betty's Enamel tinted with Lemon Yellow and apply. Using same mixture place stamens in the throat between the falls. Add touches of Cherry Red to the side of the beards. Fire at 016 or hotter. Again I would recommend practicing on the plastic overlays before attempting to start you painting.

SUPPLIES USED:

All purpose Betty's ART-AIDE mixing and painting medium.
Brushes: 3/4" Shader, #1 Liner, #10/0 Liner.
Colors: Lemon Yellow, Corn, Pretty Pink, Mallard, Pretty Violet, Azure Blue, Old Gold Green, Cream, Black Green, Olive Green, Chartreuse, Chrome Green, Cherry Red, Sapphire Blue and Betty's Enamel.

B. Humphrey

B. Humphrey

NAME

Street No.

B. Humphrey

B. Humphrey

24

B. Humphrey

B. Humphrey

28

B. Humphrey

Even Load of Color

Comma **Base** **Diamond** **Petal**

Side Load of Color

Joined Diamond

Filtered Background

Slip and Slide Brush Strokes

Violets Wipe Out With Finger

Sepals

Slip and Slide Brush Strokes

B. Humphrey

Filtered
Background

Petal
Separation

Hints and Helps
for One Time Painting

This has become an acceptable technique for china painters, in lieu of, the traditional methodology of numerous firings. To facilitate the one fire technique, I feel these points will be most helpful:

(1) The equivalent amount of paint is applied in the first painting as you would in several paintings in the traditional style. This wet on wet painting is accomplished by using transparent rather than opaque colors.

(2) Mix and paint with the same medium. Paints should be mixed very dry.

(3) Drier paints will permit use of more "all purpose meduim," which will allow more absorption of paint into the brush. Use only an "all purpose medium" that will not crawl or run during firing.

(4) More medium permits an easier application of wet on wet colors.

(5) Consistency of your painting should be such that it will "glisten" without "puddling."

(6) Using more medium will allow a greater build up and texturing which will flatten and not chip during firing.

(7) My experience has been that a hot firing (015 or 014) will better mature the colors and draws the colors into the glaze.

Glossary of Terms

"Base" stroke:
: A stroke formed with a square shader. The brush is held nearly perpendicular, lightly touching the surface with the full width of the brush, then pulling the brush toward yourself.

"Diamond" stroke:
: A stroke formed with a square shader. Holding the brush at an angle with slightly more pressure on the left side of the brush, pull the brush toward yourself and slightly to the right as you slide the brush smoothly off the surface.

Medium:
: The liquid agent used to facilitate the application of paint to the porcelain. Also used for mixing the powder colors.

Side load:
: A load to the left side of the square shader. Work the color into the brush so that it is heavier on the left than it is on the right. If multiple colors are listed the first would be loaded across the entire brush, the second color would be loaded across the left half of the brush and the third color would be loaded across the left third of the brush. If a fourth color is mentioned it would only be on the left corner of the brush.

Wash:
: A light and thin application of colors.

Wet on wet:
: Painting wet colors over wet colors before firing.

One fire technique:
: A method of starting and completing a painting with one application.

Transparent colors:
: Colors that allow underlying colors to show through. When applying one color over another, choose the most transparent colors possible.

Opaque colors:
: Colors that do not allow underlying colors to show through.